CALIFORNIA REPUBLIC

D0264751

Flags
of the World

First published in 2010 by Young Reed
an imprint of New Holland Publishers (Australia) Pty Ltd
Sydney • Auckland • London • Cape Town

www.newholland.com.au

1/66 Gibbes Street Chatswood NSW 2067 Australia
218 Lake Road Northcote Auckland New Zealand
86 Edgware Road London W2 2EA United Kingdom
80 McKenzie Street Cape Town 8001 South Africa

National Library of Australia Cataloguing-in-Publication Data:

Ellis, Julie.

Flags of the world / Julie Ellis

    ISBN 9781921580017 (hbk.)

Includes bibliographical references and index.

    1. Flags 2. History 3. Juvenile literature.

    929.92

Publisher: Diane Jardine
Publishing manager: Lliane Clarke
Project editor: Talina McKenzie
Proofreader: Leila Jabbour
Designer: Amanda Tarlau
Production manager: Olga Dementiev
Printer: Toppan Leefung Printing Limited (China)

10 9 8 7 6 5 4 3 2

Flags
of the World

Julie Ellis

young
reed

HOW TO USE THIS BOOK

This book is all about flags. It takes you from the Crusades and the Middle Ages, through modern flag use, and into the future with the Flag of Earth.

The contents page gives you an overview of the topics covered in this book, and the pages you will find them on.

You don't have to start at the beginning of the book. You can read the pages in any order.

The words printed in **bold type** have their meanings explained in the glossary on page 46.

There is an index on page 48.

If you want to find out more about flags, there is a list of references on page 46.

If you are interested in war, geography, history, design or even optical illusions, this book has information for you.

The study of flags is called vexillology (vex-il-lol-o-gy). If you read this book you may become a vexillologist (person who studies flags) or even a vexillographer (person who designs flags).

So what are you waiting for? Open it up and start reading!

UNCOMMON
VALOR
WAS A COMMON

CONTENTS

Left: This statue commemorates a famous flag image that shows six American soldiers raising the flag of the United States of America atop Mount Suribachi during the battle of Iwo Jima in World War II.

FLYING A FLAG

How do you fly a flag?

The best way to fly a flag is by using a flagpole and **halyard** rope. The edge of the flag is clipped onto the halyard. The flag rises up the flagpole as the halyard is pulled. The flag opens as it rises, and the wind makes it fly. There is no wind on the moon, so to make a flag 'fly' on the moon it has a wire along the top and bottom edges to hold it up.

Flying many flags together

When three flags are flown together the national flag of the country is flown in the middle. A line of more than five flags should have a national flag at each end. When flags are flown together they must be flown at the same height, and raised and lowered together.

Parts of a flag

Flags are more complicated than they look! There are lots of special words to describe all the different parts.

The correct name for a flagpole is a **staff**. At the top of the staff is an ornament called a **finial**. The flag is raised and lowered by a rope called a halyard. The edge of the flag closest to the staff is called the **hoist**. There is an upper and lower hoist.

If you divide a flag into four quarters, the two quarters nearest the staff are the upper and lower **canton**. The two quarters furthest away from the staff are called the upper and lower **fly**. The background of the flag is called the **field**. Any emblem placed on the field is called the **charge**.

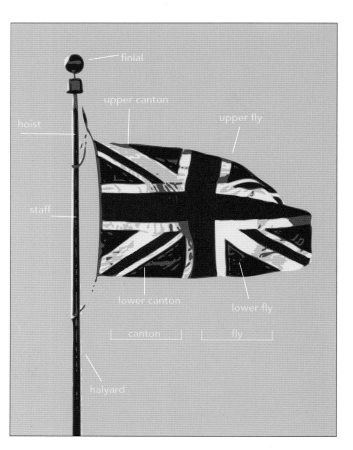

Where can you fly a flag?

Not all flags are flown from a staff. A motorcade is a procession of vehicles. Often a flag is flown from the bonnet of a car to show who is travelling, for example during a presidential or royal visit motorcade. Some people fly a flag from their house on Flag Day. In Australia Flag Day is September 3rd, in America it is June 14th, and in England it is April 23rd. Some boat owners fly their national flag from the stern of their boat, to show their nationality.

Respecting the flag

Why is it so important to respect a flag? The United States Flag Code explains that as the symbol of a living country, the flag is considered in itself a living thing and should be properly displayed and cared for. People identify with the flag of their country. To disrespect a flag is like disrespecting a person from that country.

Many people salute their flag. In the USA children learn to recite 'The Pledge of Allegiance to the Flag of the United States of America'.

The Flag Code

The United States has a Flag Code. This code outlines the proper ways to display flags. As well as the rules below, there are more rules for flag ceremonies, flying a flag inside, flags at parades or funerals, flags in schools and flags as decorations.

The Flag Code
1. Flags fly from sunrise to sunset.
2. Never fly a flag in the dark. If a flag is flown at night, shine a light on it.
3. Don't let a flag touch the ground.
4. Don't hang a dirty or torn flag.
5. Dispose of an old flag by burning it respectfully.
6. Raise the flag briskly, but lower it slowly.
7. After a tragedy or death, the flag is flown at half staff for 30 days.
8. Never fly a flag upside down except to signal an emergency.

HISTORY OF FLAGS

On the battlefield

Imagine you are a soldier on a battlefield. You are fighting the enemy in front of you, but you can't see what is happening to your fellow soldiers. Should you retreat or advance? Where is everyone? Suddenly you see the flag of your army waving to one side. You now know where to go to find your battalion.

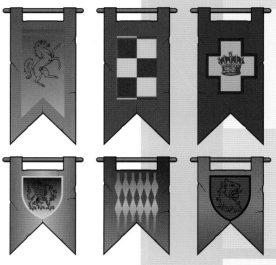

Medieval heraldic banners

A knight and his sons

You are a battle-hardened knight. You have three sons who fight with you. In your next battle you want some soldiers to follow you, and some to follow each of your sons. However, the soldiers can't tell you and your sons apart when you all have your armour on and your faces covered. You add an **emblem** to your flag. Each of your sons adds a different emblem to their flag. Every soldier can now see who he is supposed to follow.

The First Crusades

The time period from 1096–1099 was called 'The First Crusades'. Christian leaders across Europe stopped fighting each other and decided to reclaim the Holy Land back from the Moors (the Muslims). They did this by fighting their way to Palestine while carrying flags with crosses on them. Each country carried a different-coloured cross so that their country could be identified. This was an early example of national identity being linked to a flag.

A First Crusades knight

8

Flag design

The oldest flag design still in use is the Danish flag, which has an off-centre cross on it.

A diagonal (x-shaped) cross is called a **saltire**. Some flags have a serrated edge, or are divided into four equal quarters. The **bicolour** (two equal colours) and **tricolour** (three equal colours) are common designs. Some flags use a triangle of colour (usually at the hoist). Other flags have a different-coloured border. The Union Jack flag is **counter-changed**, which means two colours change on each side of a line.

Above: Danish cross
Below left: Netherlands tricolour, Below right: Palestinian flag

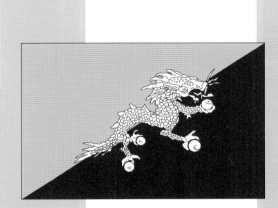

Above: Flag of Bhutan
Below left: Flag of Zambia, Below right: Flag of Uganda

Animals on flags

Animals were originally used on flags as an emblem of a group, for example, the Roman eagle. An animal on a flag is described according to the way in which it is standing, and which way it is facing. The flag of Bhutan shows a dragon **sinister** (looking towards the fly) clasping jewels in its claws. The flag of Zambia shows an eagle **volant** (flying). The flag of Uganda shows a crane **passant** (walking).

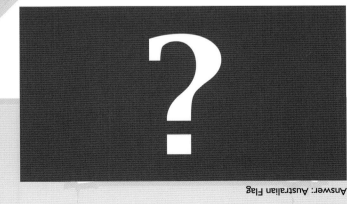

Answer: Australian Flag

The rules of heraldry

The rules of heraldry set out how flags can be designed. It is important these rules are followed because flags are officially identified by their written description.

This description is called a **blazon**. Which flag is the following blazon describing?

"The flag is a **defaced Blue Ensign**, a blue **field** with the Union Jack in the **canton** (upper hoist quarter), and a large white seven-pointed star known as the Commonwealth Star in the lower hoist quarter. The fly contains a representation of the Southern Cross constellation, made up of five white stars—one small five-pointed star and four larger seven-pointed stars."

HOW FLAGS ARE USED

Flags for protection

Flags began as a means of communication. They were useful when people could see but not hear each other. Flags then became a symbol to represent a group of people. Countries and international organisations both use flags to represent groups of people. Flags such as the Red Cross and the Red Crescent are used as a protective logo on vehicles and buildings to protect them from military attack in times of war.

Red Cross Flag

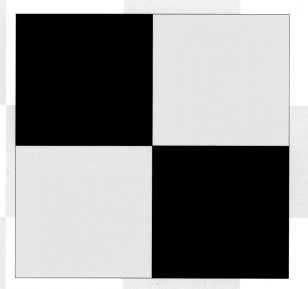

'Follow That Boat' Flag

Flags to communicate in sport

Flags are often used in sport. In soccer, linesmen, and in rugby, the touch judges, carry small flags to signal infringements to the referee. Yacht races are ruled with flags from the International Maritime Signal Flag Set. For example, a quartered flag with two yellow and two black squares means 'follow this boat'.

Flags are used to communicate in car racing. A yellow flag means slow down. A red flag means stop. A black flag means a penalty. A chequered black and white flag means it's the end of the race.

'End of Race' Flag

Flags to communicate at work

Semaphore is a way to communicate using hand-held flags. The signaller holds a square flag in each hand and moves them to different positions to signal letters of the alphabet and numbers. At sea, the flags are coloured red and yellow (the Oscar flag), while on land, they are white and blue (the Papa flag). People who work in the navy, or for the railway, use semaphore.

Semaphore signal for the letter 'P'

Nepalese prayer flags

Flags for protest or prayer

Flags can express how people are feeling. In 2008, 11 Papuans were arrested in West Papua for hoisting the Morning Star flag. This flag is a symbol of Papuan independence. The protesters were sentenced to three years' jail by the ruling Indonesians.

In Nepal, flags are used for prayer. The flags come in sets of five colours. The colours represent the elements: blue sky, white wind, red fire, green water and yellow earth. The flags are hung outdoors so that the prayers printed on them will be blown by the wind to send goodwill across the land.

Flags to represent people

People can be represented by the flag of their country. They might also belong to a sporting, political, religious or other group that uses a flag.

James Cadle, a farmer in the USA, designed the Flag of Earth. It is intended to be used for any purpose that is representative of humankind as a whole. It is not connected to any particular country, organisation or individual. It represents all of us.

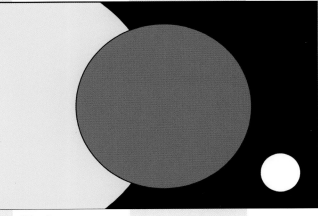

Flag of Earth

FLAGS OF ORGANISATIONS

Trade organisations

Some organisations promote trade and cooperation throughout the world.

The Association of Southeast Asian Nations promotes trade in Southeast Asia. Its blue flag represents friendship and the 10 rice stalks in the emblem represent the 10 member nations.

The European Union promotes trade in Europe. Its flag has a circle of 12 gold stars on a blue field. The 12 stars represent unity among the peoples of Europe.

The Commonwealth of Nations represents nations that are still ruled by Britain. Its flag has a dark blue field with a globe but no countries depicted. The gold lines around the globe form the letter C.

Flag of The United Nations

Flag of UNICEF

Flag of The World Organisation of the Scout Movement

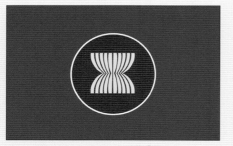

Flag of The Association of Southeast Asian Nations

Flag of The European Union

Flag of The Commonwealth of Nations

World peace

The United Nations was established after World War II to maintain international peace. Its flag shows a blue field under a simplified map of the world. This map was chosen because no particular nation is emphasised. The map is flanked by two olive branches, which symbolise world peace. Blue and white are the colours of the UN. The flag has been adapted by related agencies such as UNICEF (United Nations International Children's Emergency Fund) and WHO (World Health Organization).

The World Organisation of the Scout Movement supports young people in their physical, mental and spiritual development. The scouting world flag has a fleur-de-lis flower to show scouts they should be moving forward. The two stars symbolise truth and knowledge. The encircling rope is a reminder of the unity of all WOSM members.

Flag of the Red Crescent

Flags that help people

Red Cross and the Red Crescent help people in time of war or disaster. Their flags show a red cross or red crescent on a white **field**.

St John Ambulance teaches medical first aid and provides ambulance services. The flag of the St John Ambulance has a white eight-pointed St John cross with lions and unicorns on a black field.

Swim between the flags!

Lifeguards try to keep people safe near water. They use flags to communicate.

A red-and-yellow flag shows that the area is safe to swim in and a lifeguard is on duty. A red flag means 'danger' and that the beach is closed because the water conditions are not safe. A yellow flag means that swimmers should take extra care.

It is very important to always check the flags on the beach and stay within the marked area!

Lifeguard flags

Olympic flag

Olympic Games

The Olympic Games are hosted by a different city each time. At the end of each Games, the Olympic flag is presented to the mayor of the next host city, who displays it until the next Games. This is known as the Amherst Ceremony, and the current flag, called the Seoul Flag, has been passed around since 1988. The Seoul Flag has travelled all over the world!

The Olympic flag has a white field, with five interlaced rings in the centre: blue, yellow, black, green and red. The five rings represent the five inhabited continents of the world, while the six colours are those that appear on all the national flags of the world at the present time.

FLAGS AROUND THE WORLD

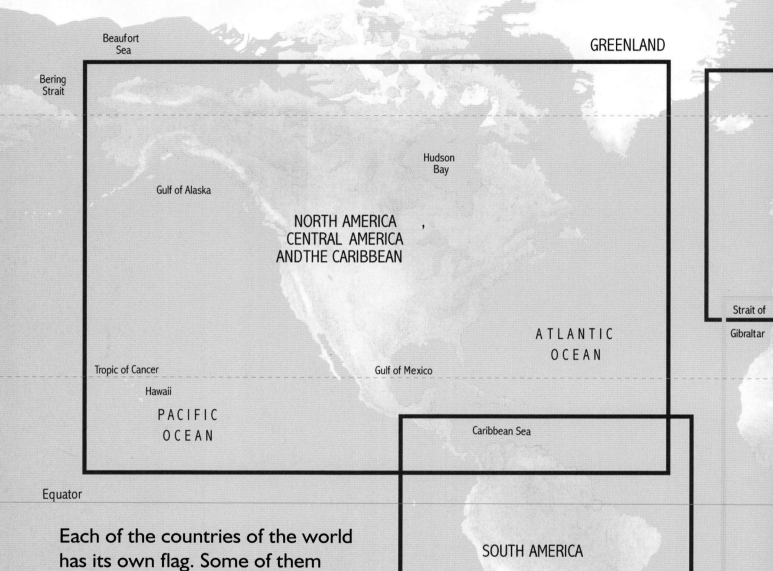

Beaufort
Sea

Bering
Strait

GREENLAND

Hudson
Bay

Gulf of Alaska

NORTH AMERICA
CENTRAL AMERICA
AND THE CARIBBEAN

Strait of

Gibraltar

ATLANTIC
OCEAN

Tropic of Cancer

Gulf of Mexico

Hawaii

PACIFIC
OCEAN

Caribbean Sea

Equator

SOUTH AMERICA

Each of the countries of the world has its own flag. Some of them have been the same for many years, while others have changed. The next section details the different flags found in each of the seven continental areas shown on this world map. You may be surprised at how some of the designs came about!

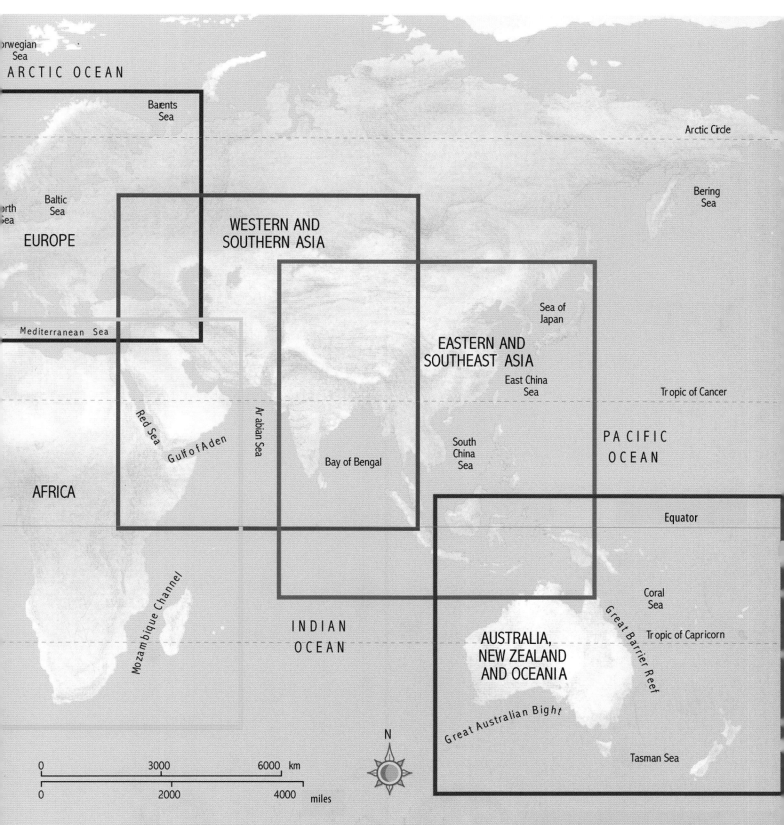

ARCTIC OCEAN

Norwegian
Sea

Barents
Sea

Arctic Circle

Baltic
Sea

Bering
Sea

North
Sea

EUROPE

WESTERN AND
SOUTHERN ASIA

Sea of
Japan

Mediterranean Sea

EASTERN AND
SOUTHEAST ASIA

East China
Sea

Tropic of Cancer

Red Sea

Gulf of Aden

Arabian Sea

South
China
Sea

PACIFIC
OCEAN

AFRICA

Bay of Bengal

Equator

Mozambique Channel

INDIAN
OCEAN

AUSTRALIA,
NEW ZEALAND
AND OCEANIA

Coral
Sea

Great Barrier Reef

Tropic of Capricorn

Great Australian Bight

N

Tasman Sea

0   3000   6000   km

0   2000   4000   miles

SOUTHERN OCEAN

The Stars and Stripes

In 1777 the United States Congress adopted its first official flag. Because there were 13 states in the union, the flag had 13 horizontal stripes and 13 white stars in the canton. In 1775 two more stars and stripes were added as two more states joined the Union. This version was known as the 'star-spangled banner'. In 1818 the number of stripes reverted to 13, to represent the original 13 states. More stars have been added, the last one in 1960 to represent Hawaii. The 'Stars and Stripes' now has 50 stars, one for each state of the United States of America.

Flag of the USA

North America is bordered on the north by the Arctic Ocean, on the east by the North Atlantic Ocean, on the southeast by the Caribbean Sea and on the west by the North Pacific Ocean. It is the third-largest continent after Asia and Africa. The countries in North America are Canada, the USA and Mexico.

Central America is the southernmost part of the North American continent.

DID YOU KNOW?

Number of countries	36
Largest country	Canada
Smallest country	St Kitts and Nevis in the Caribbean
Biggest city	Mexico City, Mexico
Highest point	Mt McKinley, Alaska, USA—6194 m (20,320 ft)
Lowest point	Death Valley, California, USA—86 m (282 ft) below sea level
Longest river	Mississippi-Missouri, USA—6018 km (3740 miles)
Largest lake	Lake Superior, Canada—82,100 km^2 (31,699 sq miles)

Flag of Canada

The Maple Leaf

It wasn't until 1965 that Canada had its own flag. It is a vertical bicolour **tri-band** of red, white, and red, with a red sugar maple leaf charged in the centre. Sugar maples are native to Canada. The length of the Maple Leaf flag is twice its width.

Canada is a bilingual country, with English and French being the official languages. This is reflected in the colours on the flag. The red is from the English Saint George's Cross, and the white is from the French royal emblem.

Flag of Guatemala

Flag of Panama

An Aztec legend

The Mexican flag is a vertical tricolour of green, white and red with the Mexican **coat of arms** charged in the centre. The green symbolises hope, the white symbolises unity and the red symbolises the struggle for freedom. The Mexican coat of arms features an eagle perched on a cactus. The eagle is clasping a snake in its beak and claw. This illustrates the Aztec legend of the founding of Mexico City.

Flag of Mexico

Central America

The Federal Republic of Central America was a democracy that existed from 1823 to 1840. The five member countries were Guatemala, Honduras, El Salvador, Nicaragua and Costa Rica. Despite the failure of the republic, all five nations fly flags that retain the old federal motif of two outer blue bands bounding an inner white stripe. Costa Rica modified its flag in 1848 in honour of the French *Tricolore.*

The other two countries in Central America are Belize and Panama. Although Belize is a monarchy and Panama is a republic, both countries use red and blue colours on their flags to represent the ruling party and the opposition.

THE CARIBBEAN

Where is the Caribbean?

The Caribbean is a region consisting of the Caribbean Sea, its islands and the surrounding coasts. It is east of Central America. The islands of the Caribbean are also called the West Indies because when Christopher Columbus landed there in 1492 he thought he had reached the Indies (in Asia).

Flag of Cuba

Flag of Puerto Rico

Spanish in the Caribbean

European colonisation of the Caribbean islands started after Christopher Columbus landed there in 1942 and claimed the entire area for Spain. These islands were later fought over by the English, the French and the Dutch. Cuba and Puerto Rico are two former Spanish colonies that show their anti-Spanish feelings in their flags. The Cuban flag has a red triangle to symbolise bloodshed and a white star to symbolise freedom. The Puerto Rican flag has red stripes to symbolise bloodshed and white stripes to symbolise freedom. The white star represents the commonwealth of Puerto Rico.

Africans in the Caribbean

Because of its climate, the Caribbean was the ideal place to grow crops such as tobacco, cotton and sugar. The invading countries of Spain, Britain, France and Holland all used slave labour. West Africans were kidnapped to be used as slaves and taken to the Caribbean. The African culture and influence is still strong in the Caribbean.

The flags of Jamaica and St Kitts and Nevis show some of the the Pan-African colours: black for the people, green for the land and gold for sunshine. The St Kitts and Nevis flag also has red for bloodshed.

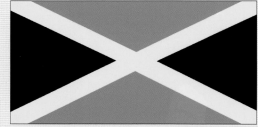

Flag of Jamaica

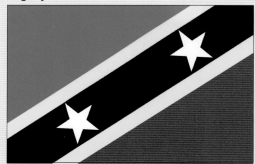

Flag of St Kitts and Nevis

Dutch in the Caribbean

In the 17th century the windward and leeward island groups of the Caribbean were conquered by the Dutch West India Company. Currently six Caribbean countries still have links to the Netherlands. They are Aruba, Curacao, Bonaire, St Eustatius, Saba and the Dutch half of St Maarten.

Each of these countries has its own flag. Bonaire, St Maarten, St Eustatius and Saba all incorporate red, white and blue in their flags to show their historic links to the Netherlands.

Flag of Saba

Flag of Cayman Islands

British in the Caribbean

British colonisation of the Caribbean began in the 17th century. By the 20th century there were eight colonies in the British West Indies. Today most countries have independence. Some countries that remain British overseas territories include Bermuda, Montserrat, Anguilla, the British Virgin Islands and the Cayman Islands. The British influence can be seen in their flags, which all have a Union Jack in their canton.

Pirates in the Caribbean

In the 17th century there were many pirates in the Caribbean. The pirates flew the **Jolly Roger** flag (also known as the skull and crossbones) to scare away other ships, and so keep their stolen goods safe.

French in the Caribbean

The term 'French West Indies' refers to the four territories presently under French sovereignty in the Caribbean. They are Guadeloupe, Martinique, half of Saint Martin and Saint Barthelme. All four countries fly the French *Tricolore*. However, Martinique also flies the 'snake flag', which is their version of the French Ensign.

French Tricolore

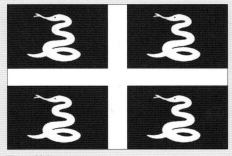
Flag of Martinique

SOUTH AMERICA

South America extends from the Caribbean Sea to the Strait of Magellan and Cape Horn. It is sometimes referred to as Latin America because of the Spanish and Portuguese influence.

Miranda's flag

Much of South America was colonised by Spain and Portugal in the early 16th century, but by 1800, people were demanding independence. In 1806 a Venezuelan called Francisco de Miranda raised a flag that consisted of equal horizontal bands of yellow above blue above red. The red represented Spanish tyranny, the blue represented the ocean and the yellow represented the new world. Venezuela, Ecuador and Columbia all adopted versions of this flag.

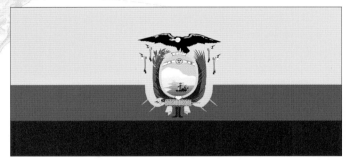

Flag of Ecuador

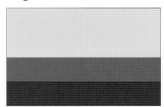

Flag of Colombia

Flag of Venezuela

DID YOU KNOW?

Number of countries	13
Largest country	Brazil
Smallest country	Suriname
Biggest city	San Paolo, Brazil
Highest point	Aconcagua, Argentina—6960 m (22,834 ft)
Lowest point	Valdes peninsula, Argentina—40 m (131 ft) below sea level
Longest river	Amazon—6516 km (4050 miles)
Largest lake	Titicaca, Bolivia/Peru—8340 km² (3220 sq. miles)

The Golden Arrow and the Yellow Star

Guyana and Suriname were both previously ruled by the Dutch; however, they are now independent republics. The flag of Guyana is known as the Golden Arrow. The predominant colour on the flag is green because much of the land in Guyana is fields and forests. The Suriname flag has a yellow star depicting unity of its ethnic groups and a golden future. Suriname was known as Dutch Guiana when under Dutch rule.

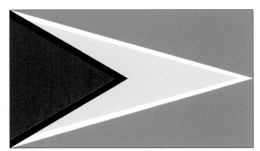

Flag of Guyana

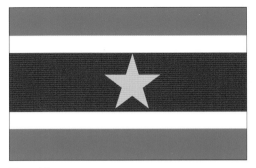

Flag of Suriname

French *Tricolore*, the official flag of French Guiana

Devil's Island

The country next to Suriname is French Guiana. It became infamous when the French government decided to use it as a penal colony. Thousands of prisoners were shipped from France to Iles du Salut and Devil's Island, two islands off the coast. French Guiana is no longer a penal colony; however, it is still under French rule. French Guiana flies the French *Tricolore*.

The largest flag in the world

Portuguese-speaking Brazil, with a population of 190 million, contains about half the people and half the land area of South America. The flag of Brazil has a green field on which a yellow rhombus is centred. A blue circle sits on the rhombus. It is inscribed with the national motto 'Order and Progress', and surrounded by 27 white stars.

The largest flag regularly hoisted in the world is the Brazilian national flag flown in the Square of the Three Powers in the capital, Brasilia. This flag weighs about 600 kg (1300 lb) and measures 7000 m² (70 m × 100 m), or 230 ft by 330 ft.

Flag of Brazil

One ancient civilisation, two modern countries

The ancient civilisation of the Incas lived in the Andes Mountains of Peru and Bolivia. Both countries were defeated by the Spanish in 1533 and became Spanish possessions. Bolivia received independence in 1825 and Peru received independence in 1826.

The Bolivian flag is a horizontal tricolour of red (for courage), yellow (for minerals) and green (for land). In the centre is the coat of arms **surmounted** by a condor.

The flag of Peru is a vertical triband with red outer bands and a single white middle band. The red represents courage and blood shed, while the white represents peace. The coat of arms in the middle contains symbols of animal, vegetable and mineral kingdoms. A military march called March of Flags is sung during flag raising.

Flag of Bolivia

Flag of Peru

Flag of Paraguay—obverse

Flag of Paraguay—reverse

Different on each side

The Paraguayan flag consists of three equal horizontal bands of red, white and blue, with an emblem centred in the white band. The red, white and blue symbolise the republic. The Paraguayan flag is unusual because its **obverse** side differs from its **reverse** side. Each side has a different emblem. The emblem on the obverse shows the state arms. The emblem on the reverse shows the seal of the national treasury.

This means the flag must be made as two separate flags and then sewn together.

The Sun of May

Argentina has a national flag that dates back to 1812. It is a triband, made of three horizontal bands coloured light blue, white and light blue. In 1818, a yellow Sun of May was added to the centre. The Sun of May symbol can be traced back to Argentina's May Revolution of 1810. The May Revolution was the start of independence from Spain. There is a legend that as the revolution was proclaimed, the sun broke through the clouds, which was seen as a good omen. The sun is also a representation of the Inca sun god Inti. It has 16 straight and 16 wavy alternating sunbeams.

Flag of Argentina

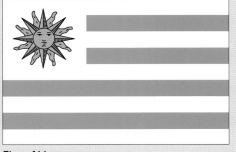

Flag of Uruguay

The sun and stripes

The flag of Uruguay has a field of nine equal horizontal stripes, alternating blue and white. The white canton is charged with a golden sun, which is the Sun of May adapted from the flag of Argentina. It represents freedom. The stripes are adapted from the flag of the USA. The stripes represent Uruguay's provinces.

The lone star

The current flag of Chile has a layout similar to the stars and stripes of the USA. Instead of red and white stripes, there are two wide red and white bands. The white symbolises snow on the Andes Mountains. The red is for the blood shed for independence. In the canton, instead of 50 white stars on a blue field, there is one lone star. The blue symbolises the sky, and the white star represents progress.

Flag of Chile

Flag of Falklands Islands

Flag of South Georgia and South Sandwich Islands

The Falklands War

There have been many wars in South America. The most recent was the 1982 Britain–Argentina war over sovereignty of the Falkland and South Georgia Islands. The war started when some Argentineans raised the Argentine flag on South Georgia Island. When South Georgia was recaptured by the British the message sent to London was, "Be pleased to inform Her Majesty that the White Ensign flies alongside the Union Jack in South Georgia." The White Ensign is the flag flown on British Royal Navy ships. Because the Falkland Islands and the South Georgia Islands are now British crown colonies, they fly the British Blue Ensign, with added emblems.

EUROPE

Countries on the border

Turkey is part of both Asia and Europe. The Bosphorus Strait, which separates Europe from Asia, runs through Turkey. Istanbul, the capital city of Turkey, is the only major city in the world that is on two continents.

Georgia, Armenia and Azerbaijan are all countries on the European–Asian border. They have recently been included as part of Europe.

Flag of Turkey

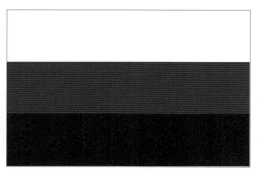

The flag of the Russian Federation
(The largest country in the world)

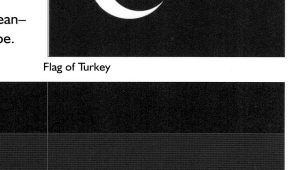

Flag of Armenia

The flag of Vatican City
(The smallest country in the world)

Europe contains both the largest and the smallest countries in the world. The largest country has a plain flag, while the smallest country has an ornate flag.

Flag of Azerbaijan

DID YOU KNOW?

Number of countries	48
Largest country	Russian Federation
Smallest country	Vatican City State
Biggest city	Moscow, Russian Federation
Highest point	Mount Elbrus, Russia—18,481 ft (5633 m)
Lowest point	The Caspian Sea—92 ft (28 m) below sea level
Longest river	Volga—3692km (2294 miles)
Largest lake	The Caspian Sea—371,000 km² (143,200 sq miles)

New countries in Europe

Since the collapse of the Soviet Union and Yugoslavia in the 1990s, many new countries have been formed in Europe. Two new countries are Montenegro, which declared its independence from Serbia in 2006, and Kosovo, which declared its independence from Serbia in 2008. Flags are very important for new countries as they represent independence.

Flag of Montenegro

Flag of Slovenia

Symbols

Many countries in Europe have a symbol on their flag. Slovenia has a shield with mountains and two wavy blue lines depicting the coastline. There is a myth that Albanians are descended from a black eagle, so their flag features a double-headed black eagle. Liechtenstein has a gold crown symbolising that it is a principality. Gibraltar has a castle and key to show Gibraltar's role in controlling access to the Mediterranean Sea. Moldova has the head of a bison to symbolise power, and an eagle to symbolise peace.

Flag of Kosovo

Flag of Albania

Flag of Northern Cyprus

Flag of Liechtenstein

Islands with two flags

The island country of Cyprus has been fought over by both Greece and Turkey. In 1974 it was divided into two parts. The northern part is controlled by Turkey and the southern part is controlled by Greece. Each part has a separate flag.

Ireland is another island country with two flags. Northern Ireland is part of the United Kingdom. It flies the Union Jack. However, the rest of Ireland (Eire) flies a tricolour flag of green, white and orange. The green represents the Catholics, the orange represents the Protestants and the white represents the peace between the two groups.

Flag of Gibraltar

Flag of Cyprus

Flag of Moldova

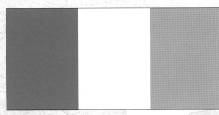

Flag of the United Kingdom

Flag of Ireland

Three flags in one

The flag of the United Kingdom (the Union Jack) is a combination of three flags: the Cross of St George of England, the St Andrew's Cross of Scotland and the Cross of St Patrick to represent Ireland.

Flag of the United Kingdom

The Red Dragon

Wales is also part of the United Kingdom but its flag is not part of the Union Jack. The flag of Wales is the Red Dragon. It is a red dragon passant, on a green and white field. Some people think the red dragon should be added to the Union Jack.

A suggested way of adding the Welsh dragon to the Union Jack. What do you think?

Flag of the Netherlands

Horizontal tricolour flags

Flags need to be easily seen and recognisable from a distance. The Dutch horizontal tricolour of the 16th century is credited with being the first 'modern' flag. Its three colours of orange, white and blue were simple and easy to see. The modern flag of the Netherlands has replaced the orange with red. Other European countries that copied the idea of three horizontal colours include Luxembourg, Estonia, Lithuania and Germany.

Vertical tricolour flags

The French flag came into being after the 1789 French Revolution. Its three vertical stripes of blue, white and red quickly became known as the *Tricolore*. The colours represent the ideals of liberty, equality and fraternity. The Italian flag was designed when Italy was under French rule, and it is a vertical green, white and red tricolour. Other countries in Europe that fly a vertical tricolour flag include Russia, Armenia, Ireland, Belgium and Romania.

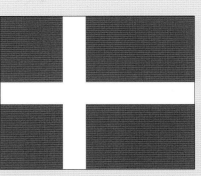
Flag of Denmark

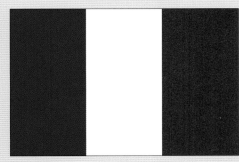
Flag of France

Cross or crescent

Some countries with a Christian background have a cross on their flag. The size and placement of the cross varies. The Swiss flag, which is an exact square, has a **couped** (cut short) cross that does not touch the edge of the flag. The **Scandinavian Cross** used by Scandinavian countries has an off-centre cross with one arm of the cross extended. Georgia has the 'Flag of Five Crosses'.

Some Muslim countries, such as Turkey, Northern Cyprus and Azerbaijan, have an Islamic crescent and star on their flags (see page 24).

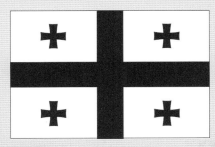
Flag of Switzerland

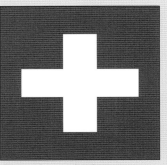
Flag of Georgia

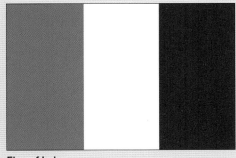
Flag of Italy

Cold land, hot flag

When Greenland was granted home rule by Denmark, a new flag was proposed. This flag shows the link with Denmark by its red and white colours; however, the circular design is unique. The white band at the top represents glaciers. The red band underneath represents the ocean. The red semicircle represents the sun (which remains above the horizon in the summer). The white semicircle represents icebergs.

Flag of Greenland

AFRICA

Where is Africa?

The African continent is the world's second-largest and second most populous continent after Asia. It extends from the Mediterranean Sea to Cape Agulhas in South Africa. It covers an area of about 30 million kilometres. Much of the land is inhospitable and difficult to travel over. One billion people (nearly 15 per cent of the world's population) live in Africa. Africa is the only continent to stretch from the northern temperate zone to the southern temperate zone.

The Pan-African colours

Green, gold and red are the colours used on many African flags. They were first used on the 1798 flag of Ethiopia. The green symbolises nature and hope. The gold symbolises the sun and peace. The red symbolises sacrifice and power. The colours were copied by other African states as they gained independence from colonisation. These colours became known as the **Pan-African colours**. Other African countries that use these colours include Senegal, Guinea, Benin, Mali, Burkina Faso, Cameroon, Congo and Rwanda.

Flag of Benin

Flag of Guinea

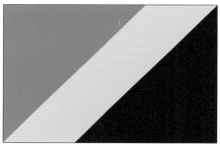

Flag of Congo

DID YOU KNOW?

Number of countries	56
Largest country	Sudan
Smallest country	Seychelles
Biggest city	Cairo, Egypt
Highest point	Mt Kilimanjaro, Tanzania—5895 m (19,340 ft)
Lowest point	Lac'Assal, Djibouti—156 m (512 ft) below sea level
Longest river	Nile, Uganda/Sudan/Egypt—6825 km (4241 miles)
Largest lake	Victoria, Kenya/Uganda/Tanzania—69,500km² (26,834 sq miles)

Better with black?

In 1957 Ghana copied Ethiopia's tricolour flag. However, the colours were flipped (red on top) and a black star was added. The black represents the people. Two other African countries that have also added black to their green, gold and red flags are Guinea-Bissau, and São Tomé and Principe.

Flag of Ghana

Flag of Guinea-Bissau

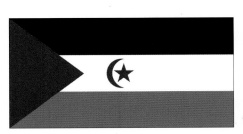

Flag of São Tomé and Principe

Flag of Senegal

Flag of Togo

Flag of Morocco

Stars

Morocco and Ethiopia both have a pentagram star known as the '**Seal of Solomon**' on their flags. Other countries also have five-pointed stars on their flags. The stars have different meanings. Senegal has a green star that represents hope. The black stars of Guinea-Bissau and Ghana denote African unity. The white star on the Liberian flag symbolises African freedom, while the white star of Togo represents peace. The Cape Verde flag has a circle of yellow stars that depict its 10 main islands. Burkina Faso, Cameroon, the Central African Republic, Sao Tome and Principe, the Democratic Republic of the Congo, Burundi, Somalia, Mozambique, Angola and Djibouti all have at least one star on their flags.

The Islamic crescent and star

Many countries in North Africa are Muslim, and so they display the Islamic crescent and star on their flags. The Western Sahara, Algeria, Tunisia and Mauritania have all incorporated the crescent and star in their flags. The islands of Comoros in southeast Africa are also Muslim. They display the Islamic crescent on their flag. The four stars represent each of the four islands.

Flag of Western Sahara

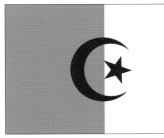

Flag of Algeria

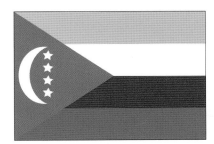

Flag of Comoros

Shields for defence

Three flags that look distinctively African are those that show shields on their flags. The Kenyan flag features a black, red and white traditional Masai shield and two spears. They symbolise readiness to defend freedom.

The central focus of the Swaziland flag is a cowhide shield with two spears and a fighting stick. They symbolise defence. The shield is black and white to show that black and white people live together peacefully in Swaziland.

The Lesotho flag has a traditional Sotho shield with a spear and ball-headed club and a plume. It symbolises the Lesotho nation's traditional safeguards for peace.

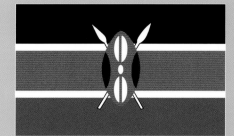
Flag of Kenya

Flag of Swaziland

Flag of Egypt

Flag of Zambia

Flag of Lesotho

The Eagle of Saladin and other birds

The Egyptian flag shows a stylised gold eagle known as the 'Eagle of Saladin'. Saladin was a great Muslim leader in the 12th century. The design is based on a carving of an eagle found on a wall in Cairo, which was built by Saladin. Birds are also found on other African flags. Zambia has an eagle, Zimbabwe has a stone bird, St Helena has a wirebird and Uganda has a crested crane.

Flag of Uganda

Green for nature

Green is the colour of the Islamic religion, and a colour that represents nature. It features on many African flags. The Libyan flag consists of a plain green field with no other details. Many African flags are tricolours with one green panel. They include The Gambia, Sierra Leone, Cote d'Ivoire, Nigeria, Gabon and Madagascar.

The flags of Tanzania and Sudan feature green triangles. The South African flag has a green pall (Y pattern). Other African flags also have green on them.

Flag of Libya

Plants

Two African countries that feature plants on their flags are Eritrea and Equatorial Guinea. Eritrea features a golden olive branch surrounded by an olive wreath. The olive wreath symbolises peace.

Equatorial Guinea is a tiny country that incorporates five offshore islands. Its coat of arms features a silver shield with a silk-cotton tree. The tree symbolises the country's historical link with Spain. It was under a similar tree that a treaty was signed with the Spanish at the time of colonisation.

Flag of Eritrea

Flag of Equatorial Guinea

Flag of Malawi

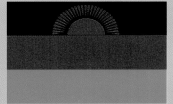

Flag of Rwanda

Flag of Niger

Flag of Namibia

Suns

Africa is a hot continent dominated by the sun. A number of African flags feature a sun on them. The gold sun on the flag of the Republic of Namibia represents life and energy. The Rising Sun on the Malawian flag represents hope and freedom. The flag of Niger has an orange circle that represents the sun. The Rwandan flag has a sun to symbolise unity.

Flag of Chad

Flag of Mauritius

Shades of blue

Blue is a common colour in African flags. It usually represents the sky, the sea or water. The blue in the Chad tricolour represents the sky. The flag of Mauritius has a blue band to represent the Indian Ocean. The pale blue on the Botswana flag represents rain, which is a precious commodity in this hot, dry country.

Flag of Botswana

Religious symbols

Western Asia is an area of historic importance for different religious groups. Many countries in this area have religious symbols on their flags. The cedar tree on the Lebanese flag symbolises that country's Christian community. The seven-pointed star on the Jordanian flag represents the seven verses that open the Muslim Koran. The Israeli flag contains the six-pointed Jewish version of the 'Seal of Solomon' star. The Saudi Arabian flag contains Muslim religious writing in Arabic. Pakistan and the Maldives both feature the Islamic crescent.

Flag of Lebanon

Flag of Saudi Arabia

Flag of Israel

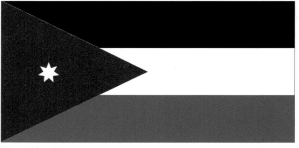

Flag of Jordan

DID YOU KNOW?

Number of countries	26 and some territories
Largest country	India
Smallest country	Bahrain
Biggest city	Mumbai (Bombay) India
Highest point	Mt Everest, Nepal—8850 m (29,035 ft)
Lowest point	Dead Sea, Israel/Jordan—392 m (1286 ft) below sea level
Longest river	Euphrates, Syria/Iraq—3600 km (2240 miles)
Largest lake	Aral Sea, Kazakhstan—62,000 km2 (24,000 sq. miles)

Pan-Arab colours

The Pan-Arab colours of red, black, white and green were first used by Arab nationalists in World War I. After the war some Arab nations used these colours in their flags. Each Pan-Arab colour originally represented a different Arab dynasty. However, Arab countries now have different explanations for what these colours symbolise.

On the Kuwaiti flag, black represents the defeat of enemies, white is for purity, green for land and red for blood. On the United Arab Emirates flag, black represents oil, white is for neutrality, green for fertility and red for the original emirates' flags. Other countries that use the Pan-Arab colours include Iraq, Palestine and Yemen.

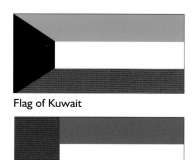
Flag of Kuwait

Flag of United Arab Emirates

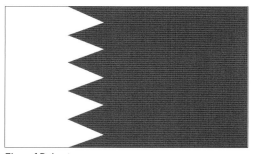
Flag of Bahrain

Flag of Qatar

A tiny Arab kingdom

Bahrain is the smallest country in Western Asia. It is made up of a group of islands that are connected to the mainland by a causeway linking it to Saudi Arabia. The white on the flag was originally a signal that it was a friendly country. The five indentations on the **serrated** line represent the five basic requirements of Islam. Qatar has a very similar flag design, which it copied from Bahrain.

National symbols

With the collapse of Russian communism in 1991, some countries formerly under Russian control became free republics. Their flags are symbols of their national identity. Turkmenistan has a band of a traditional carpet pattern on its flag. The white crescent on the Uzbekistan flag represents the new republic. The sun and the eagle depicted on the Kazakhstan flag represent freedom. The Kyrgyzstan flag shows the framework of a Kyrgyz tent.

Flag of Turkmenistan

Flag of Uzbekistan

Flag of Kazakhstan

Flag of Kyrgyzstan

20 flags for one country

Afghanistan's political changes have meant that it has had more than 20 flags since 1900.

It has had plain black. It has had plain white. It has had both vertical and horizontal tricolours. Some flags have had a seal, and some have had Arabic writing. The current flag, adopted in 2002, is a vertical tricolour of black, red and green, with the national coat of arms charged in the centre.

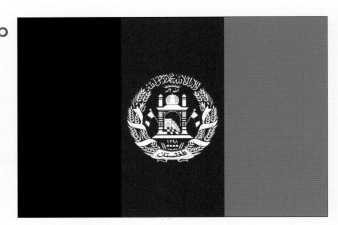

Flag of Afghanistan

Southern Asia

Southern Asia extends from Pakistan in the west through India, Nepal and Bhutan to Bangladesh and Sri Lanka. One area in northern India is disputed by both India and Pakistan, and has been halved. Azad Jammu and Kashmir is under Pakistani control. It has a population of about four million. Kashmir and Jammu is under Indian control. It has a population of about 10 million.

Each of these areas has a different flag. The green and white stripes on the flag of Azad Jammu and Kashmir represent the mountains and the valleys. The Kashmir and Jammu flag features a plough on a red background.

Flag of Azad Jammu and Kashmir

Flag of Kashmir and Jammu

The flag of a billion people

In India there are more than one billion people. There are 16 official languages. The four official religions are Hindu, Muslim, Sikh and Christian. The Indian flag is a tricolour of orange (representing courage), white (representing peace) and green (representing faith). The wheel in the middle is a chakra. To a Buddhist this wheel represents the Wheel of Law. The 24 spokes in the wheel match the 24 hours in a day.

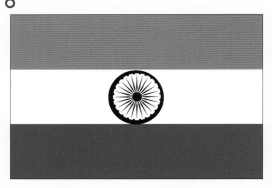

Flag of India

Flag of the Maldives

The land of a thousand islands

The Maldives is an archipelago of over one thousand small islands. It was under British rule until 1965 when it gained independence. The red on the flag symbolises the blood shed for independence. The green represents peace and palm trees. The white crescent is a symbol of Islam. Other countries to choose the red, green and white colours include Oman, Iran and Tajikistan.

The lion and the dragon

The Sinhalese word for lion is 'Sinhala', which is the basis of the name Sri Lanka. The flag of Sri Lanka features a golden lion clasping a sword. The lion signifies strength, and the sword represents authority.

Bhutan means 'Land of the Dragon', and thunder was believed to be the sound of dragons roaring. Jewels in the dragon's claws denote wealth, and the snarling mouth suggests it is protecting the country.

Flag of Sri Lanka

Flag of Bhutan

Flag of Nepal

A unique shape

Most flags are oblong or square. The Nepalese flag is based on two triangular **pennants** that represent both the Himalaya mountains and the two religions of Buddhism and Hinduism. The moon and sun originally represented the royal family and the prime minister's family, the Rana family. They also represent the country's desire to live as long as the sun and moon. The blue border signifies peace.

Eastern Asia includes China, Japan, Mongolia, Taiwan and Korea. More than 1.5 billion people live in Eastern Asia. The region is one of the world's most populated places, with about 131 inhabitants per square kilometre (340 per square mile).

Southeast Asia consists of the countries that are geographically south of China, east of India and north of Australia. It includes countries such as Vietnam, Cambodia, Laos, Thailand, Malaysia, Indonesia, Singapore and Brunei.

Flag of China

Civil war

China is a huge area with an enormous population. It has had many rulers and many civil wars. The last civil war was in 1949 when the communists took over power. The defeated nationalists fled to the island of Taiwan. Taiwan became a separate state of China. China's official name became the 'People's Republic of China'. Taiwan's official name is the 'Republic of China'. However, when competing at the Olympic Games Taiwan is not allowed to compete under the name of 'Republic of China'. Taiwan has a special 'Chinese Taipei Olympic Flag' just for use at the Olympic Games.

Flag of Taiwan

DID YOU KNOW?

Number of countries	20
Largest country	China
Smallest country	Singapore
Biggest city	Seoul, Korea
Highest point	Mt Everest, Tibet—8850 m (29,035 ft)
Lowest point	Turpan Basin, China—154 m (505 ft) below sea level
Longest river	Yangtze, China—6380 km (3965 mi)
Largest lake	Tonle Sap, Cambodia—2700 km (1042 sq. miles) in dry season

The sun

A common emblem on flags in Eastern and Southeast Asia is the sun. The sun symbolises many things, such as life, goodness, light, freedom and happiness. It appears white (Taiwan), red (Japan) or gold (Philippines) on different flags.

Flag of Japan

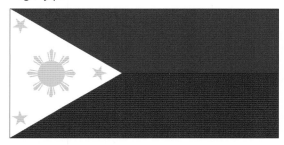

Flag of the Philippines

Little neighbours

China is the largest country in Eastern Asia. Three of China's little neighbours are Tibet, Hong Kong and Macau. Tibet is a separate region of China in the Himalayan Mountains. It has its own flag, which symbolises snow-clad Himalayan Mountains and Buddhist ideals. Hong Kong is an island that was returned to China by the British in 1997. Both Hong Kong and Macau are special administrative regions of China. Hong Kong adopted a new flag in 1997 that shows the white flower of the bauhinia tree and five stars, which copy the Chinese flag. 63 kilometres (37 miles) south-west of Hong Kong is the Macau Peninsula. It has a green flag with a three-leafed lotus flower. Under the flower a stylised bridge indicates the inseparable contact with mainland China.

Flag of Mongolia

An ancient symbol

The Mongolian flag features an ancient symbol called the 'Soyombo'. The uppermost part of the symbol is a flame above a sun and crescent moon. Inverted triangles are ancient Mongol symbols for death. Horizontal panels indicate watchfulness, and two stylised fish make up the Chinese yin-yang symbol. Two vertical columns express the old proverb that 'the friendship of two men is stronger than stone walls'.

Flag of Tibet

Flag of Hong Kong

Flag of Macau

A country still at war

After World War II the Kingdom of Korea was divided into two countries: North Korea, which was controlled by Russia, and South Korea, controlled by the United States of America. The Russians invaded South Korea in 1950. The USA protected the south and the war ended in 1953. A demilitarised zone 4 kilometres (2.5 miles) wide was created between the two countries. Because no peace treaty was signed, these countries are considered to be still at war. The North Korean flag features a communist star on a white disc. The South Korean flag features a red and blue yin-yang disc bordered by four groups of black bars (Chinese tri-grams).

Flag of North Korea   Flag of South Korea

Flag of Singapore

A tiny country

Singapore is the smallest country in Southeast Asia. It has an area of only 641 square kilometres (248 square miles) yet it contains four million people. When Singapore gained self-government from Britain in 1959 it saw itself as a young and growing nation. These ideals are depicted in its flag. The white crescent symbolises the young and growing nation. The five white stars stand for equality, justice, democracy, peace and progress.

Red, white and blue

Different countries often use the same colours on their flags, but give those colours different symbolic meanings. The flag of the Kingdom of Thailand shows five horizontal stripes in the colours red, white and blue. The three colours stand for nation, religion and king. The flag of Malaysia has a field of 14 alternating red and white stripes and a blue canton. The stripes represent the equal status of the 13 states with the federal government. The blue represents Malaysia's links to the Commonwealth. The flag of Myanmar (Burma) has a red field and a blue canton with a white star. The red signifies courage, the blue peace, and the white star purity.

Flag of Thailand

Flag of Malaysia

Flag of Myanmar (Burma)

Flag of Vietnam

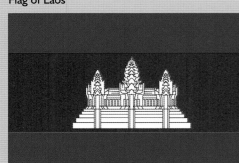

Flag of Laos

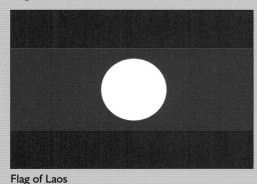

Flag of Cambodia

French Indochina

The French ruled over Vietnam, Laos and Cambodia (known as French Indochina) from 1885 until 1953. When these countries gained their independence back from France, all three put symbols on their flags that represented their individual countries. Vietnam became a socialist republic and put a five-pointed star on its flag. The points of the star represent the unity of workers, peasants, intellectuals, traders and soldiers in building socialism. The flag of Laos contains a white disc that symbolises the ruling Lao People's Revolutionary Party. The Cambodian flag depicts the ancient Cambodian temple of Angkor Wat. It is the only flag in the world that has a building in its design.

Flag of Brunei

City of peace

Brunei is a small monarchy in Southeast Asia. Its flag has a coat of arms on a yellow field. The field is cut by diagonal black and white bands. The coat of arms has a crescent (symbolising Islam) joined with an umbrella (symbolising the monarchy). Two hands symbolise government protection. Below the crescent is a scroll. On the scroll in Arabic are the words 'Brunei City of Peace'.

Gaining independence

Indonesia was a Dutch colony from 1816 until 1945 when independence was proclaimed. The 1945 flag was based on the colours used by a 13th-century Indonesian empire. The flag symbolises the complete person (red for the body and white for the soul).

East Timor became independent from Indonesia in 2002. Its 2002 flag contains symbolic colours. Black symbolises colonisation, yellow symbolises the struggle for independence, red symbolises the blood shed for independence and white symbolises peace.

Flag of Indonesia

Flag of East Timor

AUSTRALIA, NEW ZEALAND AND OCEANIA

Official flags

The official flag of Australia is based on the British Blue Ensign, with the addition of the stars of the Southern Cross and the Commonwealth star. In 1995, both the Aboriginal flag and the Torres Strait Islander flag were also officially proclaimed by the Australian government as 'Flags of Australia'.

The Aboriginal flag was designed in 1971 by Harold Thomas, an Aboriginal artist. The colours on the flag are symbolic. Black represents the Aboriginal people of Australia, red represents the red earth and yellow represents the sun.

The Torres Strait Islander flag was designed in 1992 by Bernard Namok. The green colour represents the land, the blue represents the sea, white represents peace and black represents the people. The white Dhari (headdress) also represents the people. The star represents both the five island groups within the Torres Strait and the importance of stars for navigation.

Flag of Australia

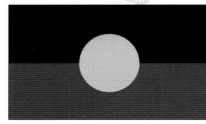

Flag of the Aboriginals

Flag of the Torres Strait Islanders

DID YOU KNOW?

Number of countries	21
Largest country	Australia
Smallest country	Nauru
Biggest city	Sydney, Australia
Highest point	Mt Wilhelm, Papua New Guinea—4509 m (14,794 ft)
Lowest point	Lake Eyre, Australia—16 m (52 ft) below sea level.
Longest river	Murray-Darling, Australia—3750 km (2330 miles)
Largest lake	Lake Eyre, Australia—8884km² (3430 sq miles)

Australian state flags   ─o

Each of the six states of Australia has its own flag, consisting of the Blue Ensign with the Union Jack in the **chief canton**, and the state badge in the fly. For example, New South Wales has a golden lion passant on a St George's Cross. Tasmania shows a Red Lion passant.

The Australian territories also have their own flags. The Australian Capital Territory shows a Southern Cross and its coat of arms. The Northern Territory has a Southern Cross and a desert rose with a black centre and seven white petals.

Flag of New South Wales   Flag of Tasmania

Flag of the Australian Capital Territory   Flag of the Northern Territory

The great flag debate

In many countries there is debate over what the national flag should look like. The New Zealand flag is based on the British Blue Ensign with the addition of the stars of the Southern Cross. Some Maori want a flag that represents them. In 2009 the Tino Rangatiratanga flag was given official recognition as the Maori flag, and on certain occasions it is allowed to be flown alongside the New Zealand flag. However, immigrant groups and others claim that New Zealand needs one flag, inclusive of all cultures, to represent all New Zealanders. There are at least five alternative designs to the current flag, but as there is no majority agreement, it is unlikely that the New Zealand flag will change in the near future.

Flag of Micronesia

⍾ White stars in Micronesia

Four islands in Micronesia—Chuuk, Kosrae, Pohnpei and Yap—make up the Federated States of Micronesia. The four stars on their flag represent the four islands. Three other islands in Micronesia have stars on their flags. Nauru has a 12-pointed star, with each point representing one of the 12 indigenous tribes on the island. The Northern Mariana Islands, and the Marshall Islands also show white stars.

Flag of New Zealand

Tino Rangatiratanga (Maori flag)

Triangles

Papua New Guinea, the Solomon Islands and Vanuatu are neighbouring nations in Melanesia that all have triangles on their flags. The flag of Papua New Guinea shows two right-angled triangles with the Southern Cross in one half and a bird of paradise in the other half. The Solomon Islands flag also has two right-angled triangles. The blue triangle represents the sea and the green triangle represents the land. The five white stars represent the five main groups of islands. The flag of Vanuatu contains a black triangle that symbolises the people. Inside the triangle is a boar tusk (a symbol of prosperity) and two fern fronds (a symbol of peace).

Flag of Papua New Guinea

Flag of the Solomon Islands

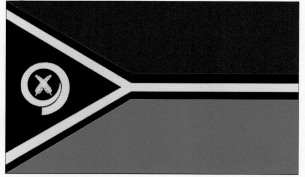
Flag of Vanuatu

Flag of Fiji

Flag of New Caledonia

Two tourist destinations

Two island groups that are popular with tourists are New Caledonia and Fiji. New Caledonia is an overseas territory of France, and so French is the main language spoken there. It flies the French *Tricolore* as its flag.

Fiji was a British colony from 1874 to 1970. The Fijian flag contains the Union Jack and a shield. At the top of the shield, a British lion holds a cocoa pod between its paws.

Flag of French Polynesia

An unofficial flag

French Polynesia is made up of several groups of Polynesian islands. They became an overseas territory of France in 2004. This means justice, education and defence are provided by the French State. The official flag is the French *Tricolore*, but they also fly a local flag with the Polynesian colours of red and white. This flag depicts a canoe sailing under a golden sun. Its crew of five represent the five island groups: the Austral, Gambier, Marquesas, Society and Tuamotu chains. The capital is Papeete in Tahiti, which is part of the Society Islands.

What's in the chief canton?

Many countries show a link to a larger territory by including a symbol in the chief canton on their flag. Tonga has a red cross to symbolise the Christianity that the British brought to Tonga. Samoa has the Southern Cross to symbolise its links with New Zealand. Pitcairn has the British Blue Ensign, with the Union Jack in the chief canton, to show Pitcairn Island's historical association with Great Britain.

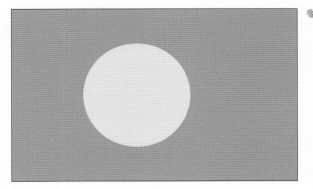

Flag of Palau

Flag of Tonga

Flag of Pitcairn Island

Flag of Samoa

Flag of Guam

A circle and an oval

The Republic of Palau has a very simple flag. It is blue with a yellow disc. The disc represents the full moon. The full moon is the best time for celebrations, planting or harvesting.

The territory of Guam has a navy blue flag edged with red. In the centre is an oval. Within the oval are a palm tree and a canoe. The tree has survived several typhoons so it symbolises tenacity. The canoe is a fast *proa* and it symbolises courage.

Birds

American Samoa is a territory of the United States of America. Its flag shows an American eagle clasping a Samoan war club and staff. The eagle indicates American Samoa's connection with United States, while the club and staff are the traditional symbol of power for Samoan leaders.

Kiribati also has a bird on its flag. It is a gold frigate flying over the sea. This symbolises authority, freedom and command of the seas.

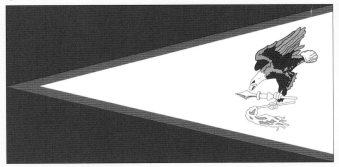

Flag of American Samoa

Flag of Kiribati

ACTIVITIES

Look in the book

Can you find these in this book?

1. A dragon passant
2. Red and white semicircles
3. An eagle volant
4. A double-headed black eagle
5. A blue wheel
6. A fleur-de-lis flower
7. Five linked rings
8. Four white snakes

Look-alikes

Indonesia used to be ruled by the Dutch. In 1945 Indonesian nationalists protested and ripped the blue stripe off the Dutch flags. The blue stripe symbolised the 'blue-blooded' Dutch aristocracy. The Indonesian flag now looks similar to the Dutch flag but without the blue stripe.

Can you find any other flags that look alike? How can you tell them apart?

Jack or Jacques?

Look carefully at the Canadian flag. Can you see the two hidden faces? The edges of the maple leaf show the profile of two angry men with long faces, their foreheads pressed together. Canada is a bilingual English/French country. The two faces are called Jack and Jacques and they refer to the English and the French Canadians. Jack is an English name while Jacques is French.

Flag of the Netherlands

Flag of Indonesia

Flag quiz

1. What are the two nicknames for the pirate flag?
2. What does 'passant' mean?
3. Which flag is nicknamed the 'Stars and Stripes'?
4. Which flag is a combination of the flags of three countries?
5. Which country has a flag known as the 'Golden Arrow'?
6. What is semaphore?
7. What does a chequered black-and-white flag mean?
8. Describe and name the French flag.
9. According the United States Flag Code, what must you do if you fly a flag at night?
10. Which flag has a yellow circle on a horizontally divided field of back and red?

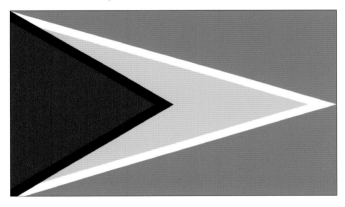

Design a flag

Design your own flag using this information.

1. Keep it simple. Another person should be able to recognise it and draw it.
2. Make it meaningful. Any colours or symbols on the flag must have a meaning.
3. Limit the colours. More than three colours and the flag will begin to look cluttered.
4. No letters. They don't reverse easily.
5. Make it unique. Your flag should not look similar to any other flag.

What is unusual about these flags?

1. Nepal
2. Switzerland and the Vatican City
3. Paraguay
4. Libya
5. Guatemala
6. Cyprus and Kosovo
7. Cambodia

Compare these flags

Which one is easier to draw and understand?

Flag of Bangladesh

Flag of St Pierre et Miquelon

WANT TO KNOW MORE?

Pocket Guide to Flags of the World by Brian Johnson Barker is a compact illustrated guide to the flags of the world.

'Flags of the World' is the Internet's largest site devoted to vexillology (the study of flags).
Here you can read more than 43,000 pages about flags and view more than 82,000 images of flags.
http://flagspot.net/flags

The CIA website has short descriptions of the flags of all countries listed in the CIA *World Factbook*.
https://www.cia.gov/library/publications/the-world-factbook/docs/flagsoftheworld.html

Wikipedia contains everything you need to know about flags, including up-to-date information about the status of countries seeking independence.
http://en.wikipedia.org/wiki/Flags_of_the_World

Purpose Games has an interactive game to practise identifying flags around the world.
http://www.purposegames.com/ww-search.php?q=flags

GLOSSARY

Bicolour: a flag with two bands of colour, either vertical or horizontal.
Blazon: official written description of a flag.
British Blue Ensign: navy blue flag with the Union Jack in the upper canton.
Canton: two quarters of a flag nearest to the staff.
Charge: an emblem placed on the field.
Chief canton: upper left quarter of a flag.
Coat of arms: heraldic insignia of an individual, family or country.
Counter-changed: two colours alternating either side of a line on a flag.
Couped: cut short, e.g. the Swiss cross is couped.
Defaced: any emblem added to the field of the flag.
Emblem: a symbolic picture.
Field: background of a flag.
Finial: ornament on top of a flag staff.
Fly: two quarters of a flag furthest from the staff.
Halyard: rope used to raise or lower flag.
Hoist: edge of the flag closest to the staff.
Jolly Roger: the name of the pirate flag, also known as the skull and crossbones.
Obverse: the face, or more important side, of a flag; where the hoist is to the observer's left.
Pall: Y-shaped pattern on a flag.
Pan-African colours: green, gold, red and sometimes black.

Pan-Arab colours: red, black, white and green.
Passant: walking.
Pennants: small triangular flags.
Reverse: the back, or reverse side, of a flag; where the hoist is to the observer's right.
Saltire: diagonal (X-shaped) cross stretching from corner to corner of a flag.
Scandinavian Cross: also called the Nordic cross, it is an off-centre cross with one long arm, commonly used by Scandinavian countries.
Seal of Solomon: there are two versions of this star. It is a five-pointed pentagram on the Moroccan and Ethiopian flags, and a six-pointed hexagram on the Israeli flag.
Semaphore: a way to communicate using flags.
Serrated: divided with a zigzag line.
Sinister: looking towards the fly.
Staff: flagpole.
Surmounted: when one charge is placed above or at the top of another.
Tri-band: another term for tricolour.
Tricolore: the name of the French tricolour flag.
Tricolour: a flag with three bands of colour either vertical or horizontal.
Union Jack: the flag of the United Kingdom.
Volant: flying.

ACTIVITY ANSWERS

Look in the book
1) Wales (pg 26)
3) Zambia (pg 9)
5) India (pg 34)
7) Olympics (pg 13)

2) Greenland (pg 27)
4) Albania (pg 25)
6) Scouts (pg 12)
8) Martinique (pg 19)

Jack or Jacques?

Look-alikes

Mexico/Italy	Monaco/Indonesia	Colombia/Equator/Venezuela
Chad/Romania	Andorra/Moldova	France/Czech Republic/Netherlands
Guinea/Mali	Haiti/Liechtenstein	Australia/New Zealand
Malaysia/USA	Slovenia/Slovakia	Luxembourg/Netherlands
Bahrain/Qatar	Cote d'Ivoire/Ireland	Costa Rica/Thailand
Russia/Moldova	Cameroon/Senegal	El Salvador/Nicaragua

Flag quiz
1. Jolly Roger, skull and crossbones (pg 19).
2. Walking (pg 9).
3. The flag of the USA (pg 16).
4. Union Jack (pg 26).
5. Guyana (pg 21).
6. A way to communicate using hand-held flags (pg 11).
7. End of the race (pg 10).
8. *Tricolore.* Three vertical stripes of blue, white and red (pg 17).
9. Shine a light on it (pg 7).
10. The Australian Aboriginal flag (pg 40).

What is unusual about these flags?
1. The flag of Nepal (pg 35) is the shape of two stacked triangles.
2. The flags of Switzerland (pg 27) and the Vatican City (pg 24) are exact squares.
3. Paraguay (pg 22) has a flag with a reverse side that is different from its obverse side.
4. Libya (pg 30) has the only national flag in the world with just one colour and no other details.
5. Guatemala (pg 17) has two antique rifles on its flag. Mozambique also includes a gun on its design: an AK 47.
6. The flags of Cyprus (pg 25) and Kosovo (pg 25), along with Christmas Island, are the only national flags that depict the shape of the country they represent.
7. The Cambodian flag (pg 39) is the only national flag in the world that has a building in its design.

INDEX

Image credits

pp1   Danie Nel (NHUK)
pp2-3   Graeme Gillies (NHIL)
pp4   Michael G Smith
pp6a   Per Palmkvist Knudsen
pp6b   Graeme Gillies (NHIL)
pp6c   Chris Breeze
pp7a   Stephen Finn
pp7b   Lance Cpl. Jeremy Ware
pp7c   U.S. Airforce photo by Staff Sgt.
        Samuel Morse

pp8a   Hypedesign
pp8c   Maisei Raman
pp9c   Royalboil
pp10a   Denelson
pp10b   Arieh
pp13b   Graeme Gillies (NHIL)
pp19a   Manueil Strehl

All other flag images: Lovell Johns, Oxford, UK
All maps supplied by Lovell Johns, Oxford, UK